FEB   2008

MACHINES AT WORK

At a Construction Site

IAN GRAHAM

QEB Publishing

First published in the United States in 2006 by
QEB Publishing Inc.
23062 La Cadena Drive
Laguna Hills, CA 92653
www.qeb-publishing.com

Library of Congress Control Number: 2005911012

ISBN 978-1-59566-191-3

Written by Ian Graham
Designed by Calcium
Editor Sarah Eason
Fold-out illustration by Ian Naylor
Picture Researcher Joanne Forrest Smith

Publisher Steve Evans
Editorial Director Jean Coppendale
Art Director Zeta Davies

Printed and bound in China

3 1518 01228 8118

Picture credits
Key: t = top, b = bottom, c = center, l = left, r = right, FC = front cover

Words in **bold** can be found in the Glossary on page 34.

CONTENTS

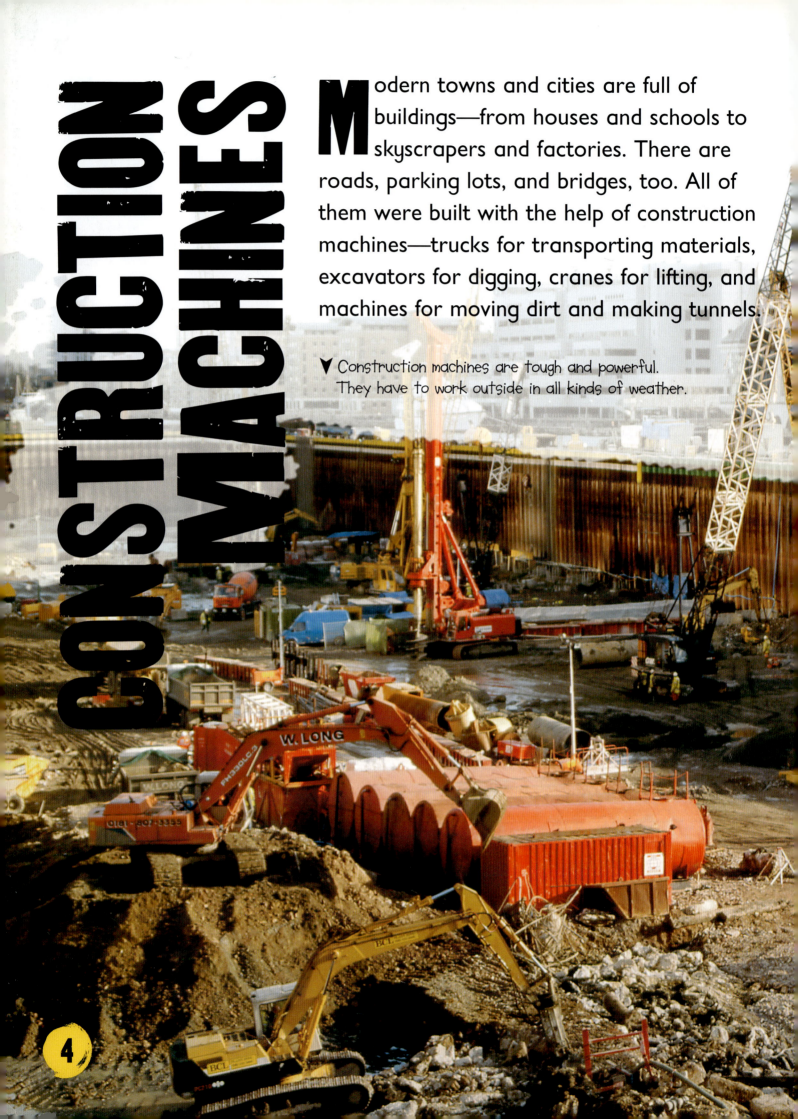

CONSTRUCTION MACHINES

Modern towns and cities are full of buildings—from houses and schools to skyscrapers and factories. There are roads, parking lots, and bridges, too. All of them were built with the help of construction machines—trucks for transporting materials, excavators for digging, cranes for lifting, and machines for moving dirt and making tunnels.

▼ Construction machines are tough and powerful. They have to work outside in all kinds of weather.

Machine power

Lots of dirt has to be moved to build modern roads, bridges, and buildings. In the past, large numbers of people did this groundwork, and it took a long time. Today, the power of machines makes it possible to do this type of work in a fraction of the time.

Many modern construction projects ➤ would not be possible without construction machines.

THROUGH THE AIR

A big construction site is a jumble of machines, materials, and workers. Everywhere are piles of dirt, sand, and gravel. The quickest way to move heavy materials around the site is to lift them up and carry them through the air. Big construction sites have many cranes for this work.

▲ Tall cranes tower high above a construction site.

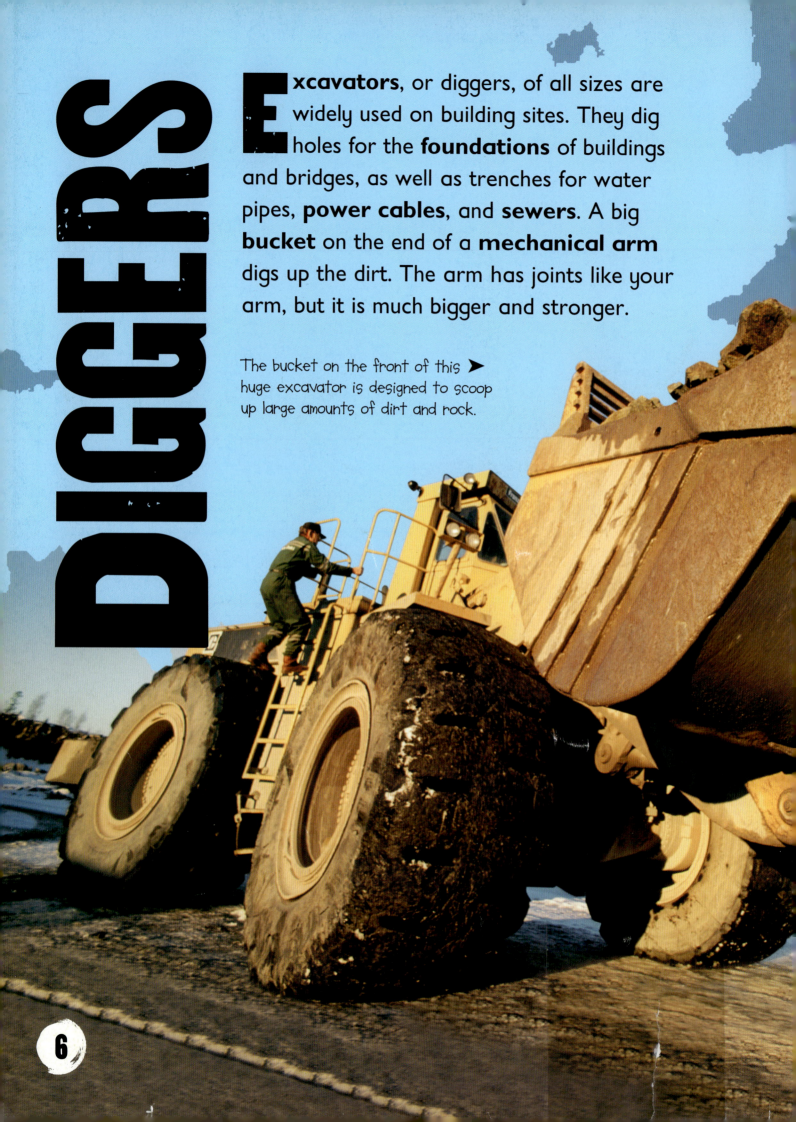

DIGGERS

Excavators, or diggers, of all sizes are widely used on building sites. They dig holes for the **foundations** of buildings and bridges, as well as trenches for water pipes, **power cables**, and **sewers**. A big **bucket** on the end of a **mechanical arm** digs up the dirt. The arm has joints like your arm, but it is much bigger and stronger.

The bucket on the front of this ➤ huge excavator is designed to scoop up large amounts of dirt and rock.

The seat of this ➤ excavator turns around to face the back when the backhoe is in use.

backhoe

Digging backwards

The **backhoe** is one of the most popular digging machines on construction sites. It has a big, wide shovel at the front for scooping up earth and other loose materials. It also has a small bucket (or backhoe) at the back for digging.

MINI-DIGGERS

A **small** skid steer loader is used for work in tight spaces where no other diggers can go. It steers by stopping the wheels or track on one of its sides. This acts like a brake and pulls the machine around into a tight turn.

A skid steer loader is one of the ▲ smallest digging machines available.

CONCRETE MIXERS

Huge amounts of concrete are used on a construction site. Concrete is a mixture of sand, gravel, cement, and water. It can be poured, molded, and spread, and it sets rock hard. Concrete is delivered to construction sites by **concrete mixer trucks**. These have a large drum on top to hold the concrete. The truck's engine slowly turns the drum, and blades inside churn up the mixture.

PUMPING OUT

If the chute at the back of a concrete mixer truck doesn't stretch to where it is needed on a construction site, a machine called a concrete pump is used. The mixer truck pours its concrete into a tank at the back of the concrete pump. The pump then forces the concrete out through a long pipe.

◄ A concrete pump carries concrete to exactly where it is needed.

▼ The drum of a concrete mixer truck must keep turning or the concrete will set hard inside it.

HTM 1204

LIEBHERR

BG·06080

Unloading

To unload concrete, the driver reverses the direction of the drum. The curved blades that mixed the concrete then turn in the opposite direction. This pushes the mixture out of the drum and down a chute at the back of the mixer.

▲ Concrete flows out of the mixer and down a chute onto the ground.

9

DEMOLITION

Old buildings often have to be **demolished** before work on new buildings can begin. Excavators can be equipped with different tools which can break up a building piece by piece.

The digging bucket ➤ of this excavator can also be used to pull down walls.

Breakers

An excavator's digging bucket can be removed and replaced with useful demolition tools. Apart from a concrete crusher, it can be equipped with a **hammer**, or breaker. Driven by high-pressure air, the hammer can smash up concrete.

▲ A concrete crusher, or **pulverizer**, can eat through walls like a metal dinosaur!

A building that took months to build can be brought down in seconds at the press of a button.

3, 2, 1 ...BANG!

Large buildings are demolished by blowing them up. Explosives are placed in the building to blow out the walls and pillars that hold it up. Then the weight of the building brings down the rest of the structure. The explosives are not all set off at once. They are set off in a carefully planned order so that the building falls down in exactly the right direction and does not damage any other nearby buildings.

EARTH MOVERS

A lot of groundwork has to be done before construction begins on a site. The ground may need to be leveled, and piles of dirt may need to be moved to build roads and bridges. Certain machines are designed to do this hard work. **Bulldozers** push big piles of dirt around, **graders** shave bumps off rough ground, and **compactors** press down loose dirt with their heavy wheels.

Dump trucks ➤ move dirt around construction sites.

FLATTENING EARTH

Bulldozers and scrapers are followed by machines called graders. These are strange-looking vehicles. A grader is like a tractor with a sharp blade underneath. As the grader moves along, the blade scrapes up any bumps of earth and stones that stick up.

▲ Graders shave the last bumps off the ground and make a flat, smooth surface that can be built on.

▼ A bulldozer scrapes up dirt and pushes it to where it is needed.

FACT!

The biggest bulldozer in the world is the Komatsu D575. Its blade is more than 24 ft. (7 m) wide (that's the length of two cars) and over 11 ft. (3.6 m) high. Bulldozers this big are called superdozers.

TUNNELING MACHINES

In the past, all tunnels were dug by men using picks and shovels. Explosives were used to blast out solid rock. Today, only the smallest tunnels are still dug by hand. The larger tunnels needed for subway trains are dug by giant tunneling machines. These machines have a cutting head at the front covered with sharp metal wheels or teeth.

A modern tunneling ➤ machine, being prepared for action, towers over the workers.

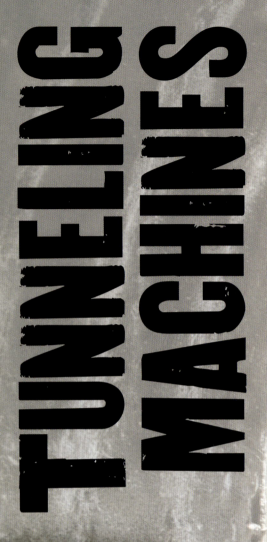

▲ Rock drills like this are powered by air instead of electricity.

Tiny tunnels

Small tunnels are too narrow for a road-header to fit inside. These tunnels are dug out with the help of air-powered drills, also called **pneumatic drills**. High-pressure air punches the sharp end of the drill into the rock many times a second, chipping the rock away.

FINISHING OFF

Even small tunnels have to be given a hard lining to stop loose rock falling into the tunnel. First, wire mesh is fastened in place all around the tunnel. Concrete is then sprayed onto it. Finally, long bolts are screwed through the lining into the surrounding rock to hold it in place.

◄ Wire mesh gives the tunnel lining extra strength.

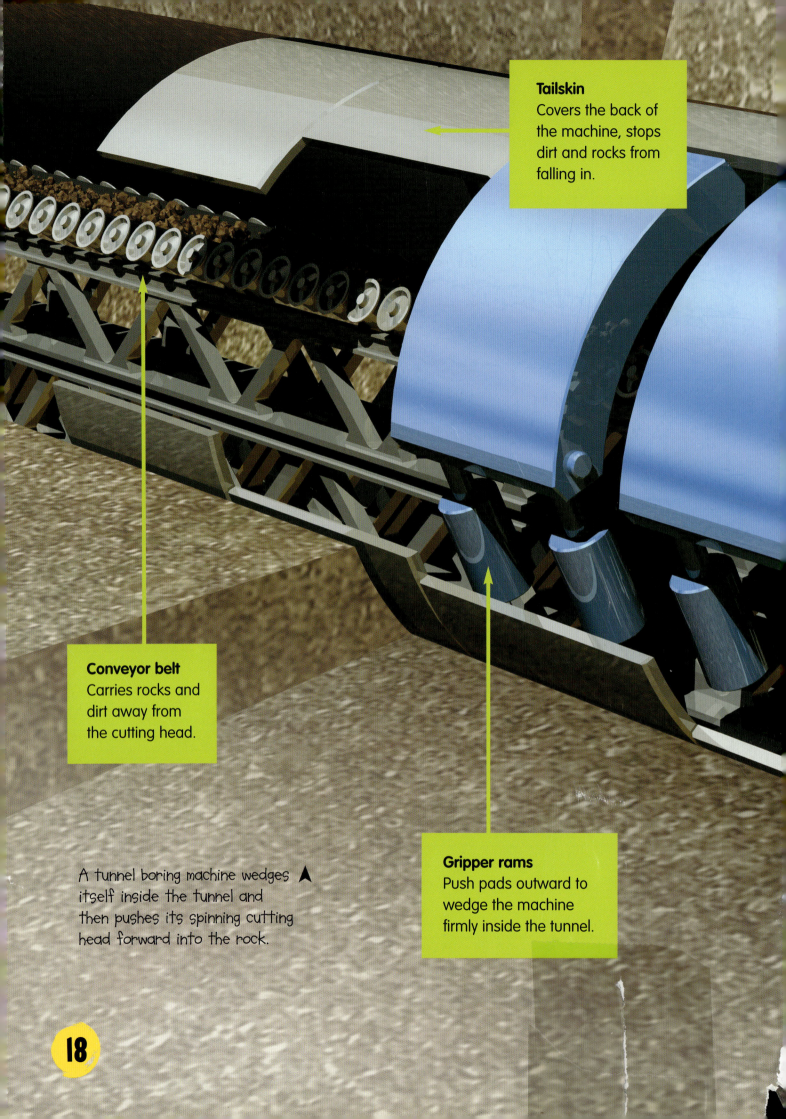

Tailskin
Covers the back of the machine, stops dirt and rocks from falling in.

Conveyor belt
Carries rocks and dirt away from the cutting head.

Gripper rams
Push pads outward to wedge the machine firmly inside the tunnel.

A tunnel boring machine wedges itself inside the tunnel and then pushes its spinning cutting head forward into the rock.

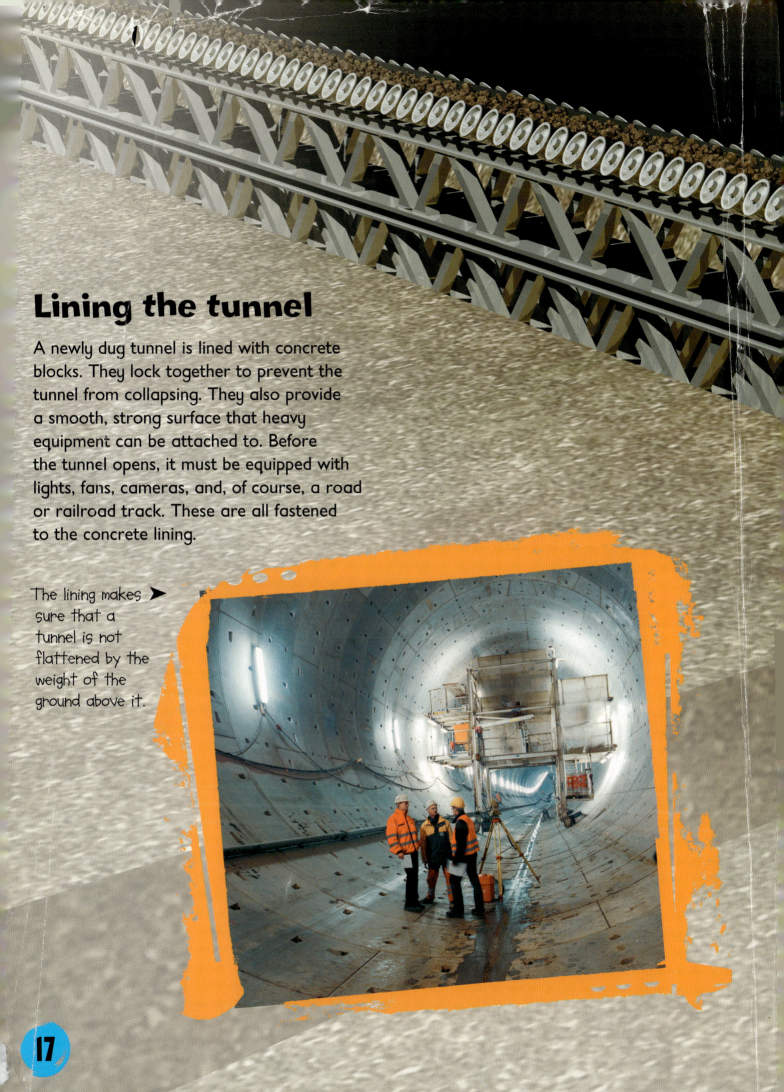

Lining the tunnel

A newly dug tunnel is lined with concrete blocks. They lock together to prevent the tunnel from collapsing. They also provide a smooth, strong surface that heavy equipment can be attached to. Before the tunnel opens, it must be equipped with lights, fans, cameras, and, of course, a road or railroad track. These are all fastened to the concrete lining.

The lining makes ➤ sure that a tunnel is not flattened by the weight of the ground above it.

MECHANICAL MOLES

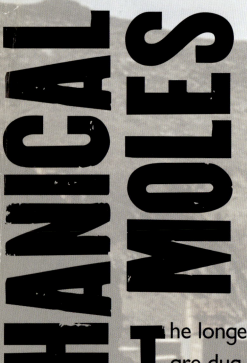

The longest tunnels are dug by special **tunnel boring machines,** or TBMs. A TBM moves through the ground like a giant mechanical mole, carving out the tunnel as it goes. The machine locks itself in one place inside the tunnel and pushes a cutting head forward to cut through the rock.

The spinning cutting head of the TBM ➤ bites into the rock to carve out the tunnel. The cutting head is covered in dozens of sharp wheels or teeth-like cutters called picks. The picks bite into the rock and carve out the tunnel.

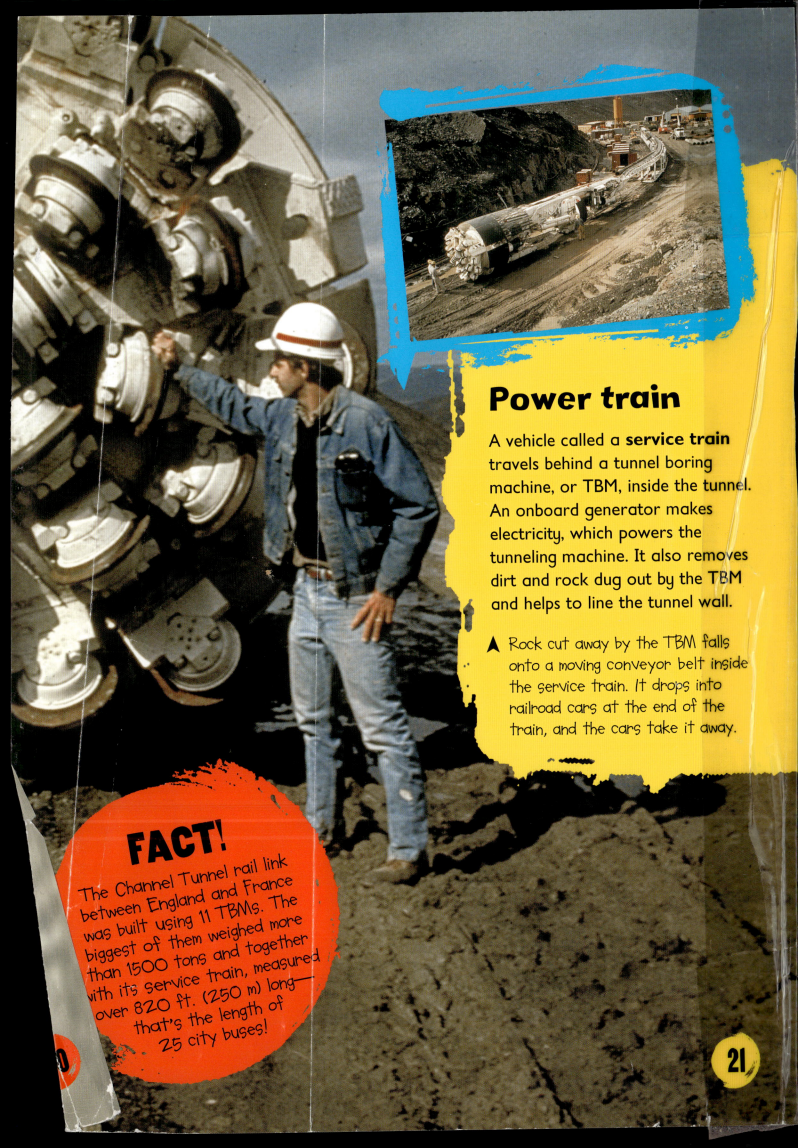

Power train

A vehicle called a **service train** travels behind a tunnel boring machine, or TBM, inside the tunnel. An onboard generator makes electricity, which powers the tunneling machine. It also removes dirt and rock dug out by the TBM and helps to line the tunnel wall.

▲ Rock cut away by the TBM falls onto a moving conveyor belt inside the service train. It drops into railroad cars at the end of the train, and the cars take it away.

FACT!

The Channel Tunnel rail link between England and France was built using 11 TBMs. The biggest of them weighed more than 1500 tons and together with its service train, measured over 820 ft. (250 m) long—that's the length of 25 city buses!

▼ A team of tunnelers stand in front of their road header tunneling machine.

TUNNEL CUTTER

Tunnels that are too small or too tightly curved for a tunnel boring machine to fit inside may be dug by a machine called a road header. Its cutting head is on the end of a boom that can move up, down, and sideways. The machine's operator steers the boom, and the spinning cutting head cuts rock away to form the tunnel.

Cutting head
Turns so that the teeth cut into the rock.

◄ The cutting head at the front of a tunnel boring machine turns up to ten times a minute. The speed depends on how hard the ground is.

Thrust rams
Push the cutting head forward and also steer the machine.

Cutting teeth
Cut into the rock.

Scraper
Scrapes loose rock away as the cutting head turns.

19

PILES OF WORK

It is very important for a building to stand on firm ground, otherwise it might lean over or even fall down! The famous Leaning Tower of Pisa in Italy leans because its weight squashes the ground more on one side than the other.

Tall buildings stand up straight today because they are built on top of long "pegs" called **piles** that are driven deep underground.

Driving piles into ➤ the ground is one of the first jobs to be done on a construction site.

pile

From the ground up

When the foundations of a big building are finished, rows of steel bars stick out from the tops of the **piles**. A grid of steel bars is then built over the piles. Then concrete is poured over it all to lock the base of the building to the piles.

◄ The steel bars that run through concrete are called rebars. This means "reinforcing bars," because the bars reinforce, or strengthen, the concrete.

BORING WORK

Another way to make piles is to bore holes into the ground and then fill them with steel and concrete. A machine called an auger bores holes by screwing itself into the ground. When it is pulled out, the dirt comes out with it. Then the hole is filled in again with concrete and steel.

▲ An auger looks like a giant screw. A motor turns it and screws it into the ground.

CRANES

Heavy materials have to be moved around on construction sites. **Tower cranes** are the machines for this job. These cranes have a metal tower with a boom, or arm, balanced on top. The load is lifted by a hook at one end of the boom. The weight of the load is balanced by another heavy weight on the opposite side of the tower.

Traveling cranes

A **mobile crane** is a crane on a truck. Before it lifts anything, legs called **outriggers** come out from its sides and push down onto the ground. These keep the crane level and make it wider so that the load it lifts will not pull it over.

boom

The Millennium Bridge in Gateshead, England, weighs around 850 tons. It was lifted into position by Europe's largest floating crane, Asian Hercules II.

hook

operator's cab

Tower cranes ➤ do all the heavy lifting work on construction sites.

UNDERWATER LIFTING

If a sunken boat needs to be lifted or a bridge has to be raised into position over a river, a floating crane may be used. This type of crane sits on top of a floating barge.

FACT!
The world's biggest floating crane is Saipem 7000. It can lift an amazing 14,000 tons!

LAND GIANTS

Many materials and products used in the construction industry are made from raw materials that are found underground. These are dug out of the ground by giant digging machines. One of the biggest of these is the **bucket wheel excavator**.

FACT!

The world's biggest bucket wheel excavator is also the biggest vehicle of any kind. The MAN Takraf RB293 weighs 14,000 tons, and each of its buckets is as big as a car!

WALKING DIGGERS

Dragline excavators have a huge bucket that dangles from a cable at the end of a long boom. The bucket is used to dig up dirt. It is lowered onto the ground and dragged toward the excavator, scraping up dirt as it goes. The biggest dragline excavators move by walking on giant metal feet.

▲ This dragline bucket holds enough dirt to fill more than 200 bathtubs.

▲ Amazingly, the biggest bucket wheel excavators weigh as much as 10,000 cars! This machine digs by using a special wheel with buckets. As the wheel turns, the buckets dig into the ground and scoop up dirt.

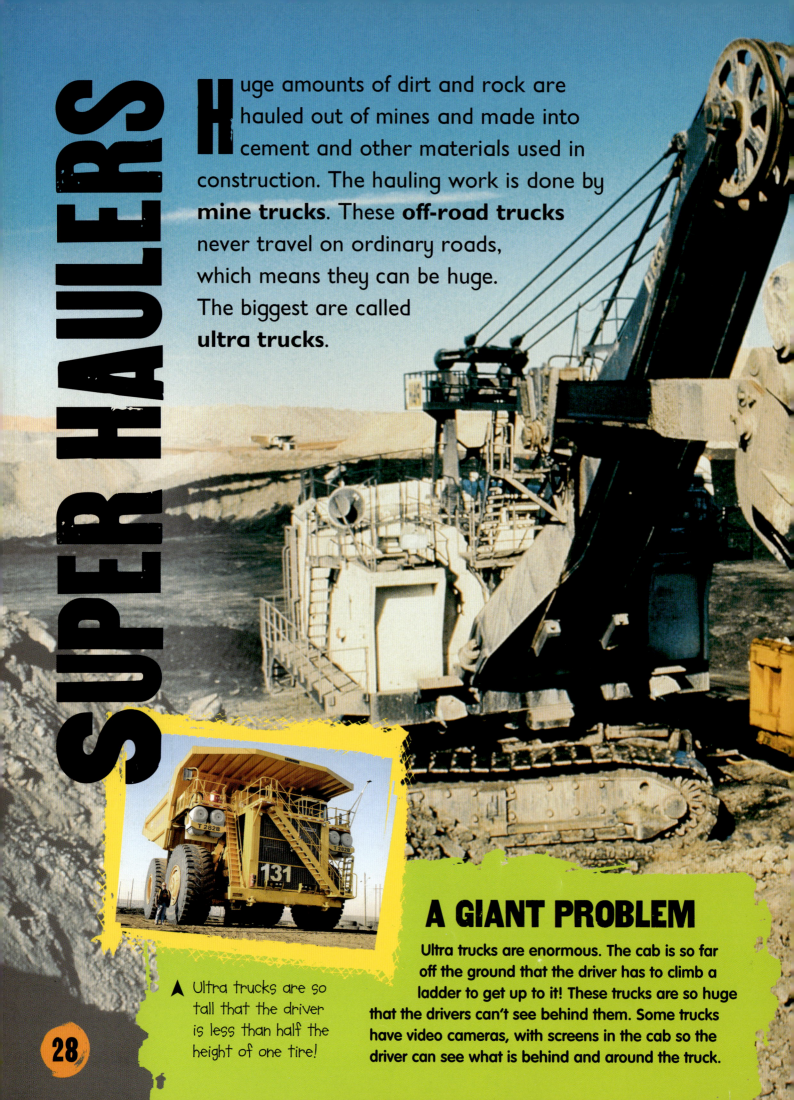

SUPER HAULERS

Huge amounts of dirt and rock are hauled out of mines and made into cement and other materials used in construction. The hauling work is done by **mine trucks**. These **off-road trucks** never travel on ordinary roads, which means they can be huge. The biggest are called **ultra trucks**.

▲ Ultra trucks are so tall that the driver is less than half the height of one tire!

A GIANT PROBLEM

Ultra trucks are enormous. The cab is so far off the ground that the driver has to climb a ladder to get up to it! These trucks are so huge that the drivers can't see behind them. Some trucks have video cameras, with screens in the cab so the driver can see what is behind and around the truck.

Unloading

Trucks empty out their load by tipping up the back of the truck so the contents slide onto the ground. The biggest dump trucks can empty out more than 360 tons of dirt in just 30 seconds.

It takes enormous power ➤ to lift the back of a full truck and empty it.

▼ The biggest trucks on Earth are used in the mining industry. Some are as big as a house.

ROAD TRUCKS

All kinds of building materials are delivered to construction sites by trucks. Loose materials such as sand, gravel, and dirt are delivered by dump trucks. These are smaller than the giant dump trucks used in mining, because they have to travel on ordinary roads. Many types of goods and materials are transported by different types of trucks. Some are **rigid** and others, called **tractor-trailers**, bend in the middle.

A dump truck ➤ transports loose materials such as dirt in a big box that can be tipped up.

Wooden platforms

Heavy items transported by truck are often carried on wooden platforms called pallets. The pallets have a space underneath so they can be lifted easily by a forklift.

Forklifts are often used to unload goods from delivery trucks.

ROAD-BUILDING MACHINES

The machines **that build roads** are called **pavers**. Small stones and a thick, black, oily substance called **asphalt**, or **blacktop**, are loaded into a paver. The machine mixes the stones and hot asphalt together. As it moves along slowly, the paver spreads the mixture on the ground to make a new road.

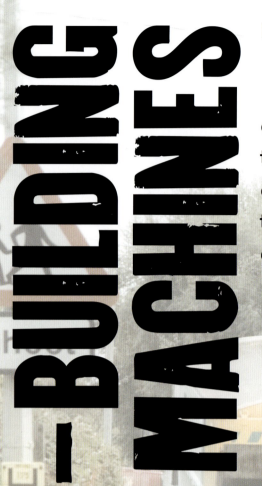

A paver spreads ▲ steaming hot asphalt mixed with small stones onto the ground.

A machine called a **roller** follows the pavement layer. ➤ As it drives up and down the road, its heavy rollers flatten and harden the newly laid road surface.

GLOSSARY

asphalt   a black substance that is used to make road surfaces

auger   a screw-shaped tool that can drill holes into the ground

backhoe   a vehicle with a scooping bucket at the front and a digging bucket at the back

blacktop   like asphalt, a black substance that is used to make road surfaces

boom   the long arm on a crane

bucket   the part of a digging machine that scoops up dirt

bucket wheel excavator   a large digging machine with a huge wheel at the front to which lots of buckets are attached. As the wheel turns, the buckets dig up dirt

bulldozer   a powerful machine with a large blade at the front that can push huge amounts of dirt

compactor   a heavy vehicle driven across soft dirt to squash it down and make it harder

concrete mixer truck   a truck that has a large, round container on its back in which concrete is mixed

conveyor belt   a moving belt that is used to move goods or materials from place to place

cutting head   a part of a machine with sharp wheels or teeth for digging through the ground

demolish   pull down or destroy

dump truck   a truck with a large open container called a box on the back, that is emptied by tipping it up

excavator   a digging machine

foundations   the bottom layer of a building. Foundations make a level, strong surface on which the rest of a building can be built

grader   a vehicle with a sharp blade underneath. The blade smoothes out bumps on the ground as the grader drives along

hammer   an air-driven tool that fits on the end of an excavator's arm instead of a digging bucket. It is used to break up concrete

loader   a vehicle with a bucket that is used to scoop dirt or other loose materials off the ground. The material is then loaded into a truck

mechanical arm   a metal arm that is worked by a machine

mine trucks   large trucks that dig up and carry materials from mines

mobile crane   a crane with wheels that can travel by road

off-road truck   a truck that works on rough ground. Some off-road trucks never travel on roads

outriggers   strong metal legs that reach out from the side of a machine or a vehicle to give it a wider base and so make it steadier

paver   a machine that lays a new road surface

piles   long metal or concrete pillars that are sunk into the ground to provide supports on which a building can be constructed

pneumatic drill   a powerful drill operated by compressed air

power cables   lengths of wire that carry electricity to a building

pulverizer   a machine that crushes something completely

rigid   something that does not bend

roadheader   a machine that makes tunnels by grinding through rock

roller a machine that flattens and hardens the surface of a newly laid road

scraper a machine that moves earth by scraping it up into a big box called a hopper

service train the railway train that follows a tunnel boring machine and provides it with power

sewer a system of pipes to take waste water away from houses and buildings

skid steer loader a small digging machine that steers by stopping the wheels or tracks on one side

tower crane a crane that sits on top of a tall metal tower

tractor-trailer a large truck that can bend in the middle

tunnel boring machine (TBM) a machine designed to cut its way through the earth to create a tunnel

ultra truck any of the world's biggest trucks. Ultra trucks are used in the mining industry.

FIND OUT MORE

Websites

Find out more about trucks, diggers, bulldozers, and other building machines and vehicles:
www.kenkenkikki.jp/zukan/e_index.html

Discover how a tower crane is built and how it works:
http://science.howstuffworks.com/tower-crane.htm

Learn all about mobile cranes:
http://science.howstuffworks.com/hydraulic-crane.htm

Read about skid steer loaders:
http://science.howstuffworks.com/skid-steer.htm

Discover the history and facts about demolishing buildings by explosives:
http://www.implosionworld.com

Find out how a building is demolished by explosives:
http://science.howstuffworks.com/building-implosion.htm

INDEX